BEING BUILT FOR US

TANZANIA BACON

Copyright © 2025 by Tanzania Bacon

All rights reserved. This book or any portion thereof may not be reproduced or used in any manner whatsoever without the express written permission of the publisher except for the use of brief quotations in a book review.

Printed in the United States of America

First Edition, 2025

PAPERBACK ISBN: 979-8-3492-9051-0

EBOOK ISBN: 979-8-3492-9052-7

Red Pen Edits and Consulting

www.redpeneditsllc.com

TABLE OF CONTENTS

DEDICATIONS 1

INTRODUCTION 3

CHAPTER ONE

    From The Beginning Of Time 9

CHAPTER TWO

    A Life I Never Planned 31

CHAPTER THREE

    Broken For The Sake Of Being Built 53

CHAPTER FOUR

    The Well Of Redemption 81

REFERENCES 93

ABOUT THE AUTHOR 95

Dedications

To Trevon and Omar,

Thank you for allowing me the incredible privilege of being your parent. This journey has been filled with ups and downs, and I am grateful for every moment we've shared. I know I have made mistakes along the way, but your grace in letting me learn, apologize, and grow has been a gift beyond measure.

You are my "WHY" in so many ways, inspiring me to be better every day. Thank you for your encouragement, for your GENTLE corrections, and for loving me with an unconditional love that fills my heart with joy.

With all my love,

Mommie

Introduction

Over the years I have gone back and forth about writing my story and opening myself up to others. I silently fought with what people would say if they knew what I did. Would they still like me? Would they even want to be around me? I wrestled with my own inner battles while imagining what people's reactions would be. After years of hiding what I had experienced, I am finally ready to share with the world all that made me who I am and who I am becoming. As I embark on this journey of making my mark on this earth, I figured it was time that the world knew Tanzania. I wanted to be able to mark the starting point by releasing this book about how God has been with me and where I am now. Some people say that they won't understand who you truly are until they know where you have been. This book is going to allow you to see that where I come from has not hindered me but pushed me to go even further and do even more in life. I am a person who is learning how to be vulnerable. I have learned over the years that vulnerability allows you to heal, and it helps others heal too. My pain was purposeful. One of my favorite scriptures says, *"It is good for me that I have been afflicted; that I might learn thy statutes."* **(Psalm 119:71 KJV)**. I know some people probably would look at me funny and say why would you say that. It took a long time for me to be okay with feeling pain. Some people run from pain, avoid pain, or compromise so they don't feel pain. However, I have learned that pain allows me to be open to healing. Healing allows me to be open to seeing the different characteristics of God. In my story, you will see how a life of pain has brought so much beauty, and it is producing great things in my life. My main purpose in this book is to encourage you to hope again in God. The pain is meant for a purpose. Some may have loss a spouse or a job or got a divorce, maybe even loss their children, or going through a custody battle. No matter what it is, the main thing is that the life you had known is no longer your reality, and you may feel hopeless. You don't see light at the end of the tunnel, and you're tired of hearing the normal church sayings or even people telling you *"it's going to get better."* I get it. I have been there. I even remember saying, *"God stop letting people pray for me because I don't want it."* I have seen dark days and even dark years to the point, where I didn't hope for anything. I made up my mind to not be hopeful, to not expect anything good. Just settle for whatever I get because I was never going to get anything good. However, I am here to encourage you to hope again in God. My prayer is that me sharing my story with you and how I took infant steps in hoping in God again will encourage you to do the same. One of the sayings that the seasoned folks use to say is *"it isn't over 'til the fat lady sings."*

Well that just isn't it. It isn't over until God says so. I have built my life by always remaining resilient and persevering no matter what the situation looks like. Keep your mind and heart open as you read. This book will be filled with a roller coaster of emotions. You may experience every emotion that is possible, but I promise you, amongst all the craziness and setbacks, there is victory and freedom! I didn't understand why I had to endure so much. As I looked at my life unfold before my eyes, I am grateful for every setback, hiccup, roadblock, and self-decision. It all made me feel better. Now, I am going to be 100% honest with you. When I was going through some of these things, my faith in God was not as strong and I didn't know a lot of scriptures.

It wasn't until I started growing in the things of God. I saw how even though I didn't know the scripture reference or have this deep relationship with God, He was with me all the time allowing His hand of grace and mercy to follow me. For that I am eternally grateful.

In each section, I want you to work through the situations that caused you to lose hope.

Write down two or three things in your life that caused you to lose hope.

_____

_____

_____

_____

_____

_____

_____

_____

_____

_____

_____

_____

_____

Ask yourself, how did those things alter your perspective on life?

Chapter One

FROM THE BEGINNING OF TIME

Born in North Philadelphia as the baby of the crew, I remember my siblings telling me a story about when I came home from the hospital. I was just so precious, and my parents wouldn't allow them to touch me. That story always confirms to me that I was the princess of the family, and I ran with it for years. My parents were so excited to have me. My dad was so excited to have a daughter. He was sitting at home watching the National Geographic Channel before coming back to the hospital to see me. They began to talk about a place called Tanzania and they showed the queen and all the beauty of the land. My dad knew at that moment that he wanted to name me Tanzania. So, my dad in his active addiction and under the influence headed to Einstein Hospital and he told my mother that he was going to name me, Tanzania Queen of Africa. Now, imagine wanting to name your child something and then they ask how to spell it, and you don't know. So, they looked it up and spelled it just like the country. Names are an important part of a kid's future. Oftentimes, as parents, we just name them something without taking into account that this will be an identifying factor for them for the rest of their lives. Tanzania - When I think about names and how much they mean, I often think about how over the years I have grown into my name. Even though my parents named me Tanzania I didn't know my name was Tanzania until I got in 3rd grade and had to take state tests. That's when I figured out what my government name was. From the time I can remember, everybody always called me *Tanzy*. That was the name I used on all my papers at school and my friends called me that. Can you imagine your teacher passing out the bubble answers sheets for the test and they say raise your hand if you didn't get one? I raised my hand, and they said, "oh we have yours, Tanzania." I was like, "who was that?", with a puzzled look on my face. I didn't know what to think. So, I just jumped up and grabbed the bubble sheet. I was in a full culture shock moment.

When I got home, I was able to have a conversation with my parents and they were able to help me process. My parents have always wanted a better life for me and my siblings. My parents experienced the streets of Philadelphia, and it had almost tore our family apart. Even though my mom was clean and sober, my dad still struggled with his addiction. After our house was shot up, my mom decided she would move us to North Carolina to give us a better future. My parents both dealt with drug addictions, and they didn't want the streets of Philadelphia to get a grip on us. They would often tell us that they did enough drugs and craziness for all of us, and they didn't want us to fall into the traps set by the streets. So, they made a hard decision and left family and friends to create a better life for their kids in North Carolina. Oftentimes, we have to make decisions that will cause us to leave everything we know and love to be better. I am forever grateful for the sacrifices that my parents made to make sure we had a better life. When we moved to North Carolina, I was young and didn't remember much. However, my siblings had to leave their friends, schools, and cousins to come to a small town in the south and start over. It was a hard transition to go from being around family and in a fast-paced city to a small city where they barely had a bus system. On top of that, we knew very little people. We moved to my grandfather's house and eventually moved to the projects. My mom was clean and sober. However, my dad was still in his active addiction. The first couple of years were hard on our family. Eventually, after about three years, my dad got clean, and our life began to get better.

I grew up in a middle-class African American family during the 90's. My parents would work two and sometimes three jobs to make sure we had all that we needed and a few of our wants. There were four kids in the home: one boy and three girls. My parents kept us fed and clothed and allowed us to go on some very special trips with our schools. My parents had very difficult lives as children. They wanted to make sure our childhood was the opposite of theirs and they worked hard every day to make that happen. My parents always wanted to ensure we were exposed to all types of opportunities, no matter what it cost them. So, as children, my parents made sure we went on all of the trips. I remember being in 5th grade and going to space camp. It was a weeklong camp in Florida, and it cost about $700 to $800. Some people would say that it is not that bad. However, back in the 90's that was a lot for a family to send one child somewhere. I remember going to the meeting and wondering how my parents were going to pay for it. I was so excited to hear about all that would take place on the trip, but I didn't want to get too excited because I didn't want to be let down. I know my parents couldn't afford to send me and I didn't see a way for them to do it. I remember the meeting ended and my mom asked about the deposit. Now if I knew anything, I knew my mom would write a check and keep it pushing. I knew my dad would be yelling about the check, but it would get paid. However, when my mom began to ask about the deposit, I overheard the person in charge tell my mom that my deposit had already been paid. My mom looked shocked, and I was too. However, as a child that was the first time I would meet this God that my mom would talk about that was a provider.

I didn't really know this God, but I knew when she prayed, He always came through so I was okay with Him. In every situation and in many circumstances, He has continued to come through. I was able to go on the trip and I had a ball. I remember several times in my youth when my mom's God would show up for me and

I would have experiences with Him. I had a relationship with Him, but it was based on my mom. I remember when I first saw angels. I was a hall patrol, and I saw these images and I asked my friend did they see it and they said, "no girl you're silly." I didn't fully understand what it was, but I knew it was a God encounter. I felt peace and the presence of God just as I did many times in church. I was a believer in God, and I went to church, not always understanding things but believing that this God that my mother and grandfather talked about so much was faithful, true and He was also real. Not only did I see things, but I also smelled things. Little did I know God was expending my capacity for Him and the things of God. I would encounter Him in so many ways as a youth. And what I thought to be impossible was that He allowed it to be so. The Bible speaks of having childlike faith. This is what I was experiencing.

I lived what others would call a normal childhood throughout my elementary and middle school years. My parents worked hard and provided a life for me and my siblings. They would attend all our events and make sure we had food, and all of our needs met. They would even work overtime to make sure we had some of our wants. In middle school, I would find my love for playing basketball and music. I played basketball and played in the band. My siblings were all high scholars, and they always set the bar high when it came to achievements. As the little sister, I never wanted to disappoint my parents. I always wanted to make sure that I was reaching all of the expectations. So, I worked hard in school and sports. I just knew by leaving 8th grade I would go into my high school career and be just as successful as my siblings had been. Little did I know, what I was about to experience was going to shake the very foundation of my life.

As a little girl, I never pictured life outside of the American Dream. My parents had done an excellent job at making me think that the pattern in life was marriage, buy a home, raise a family, go to college and then get a career, work 30 years and then retire. Little did I know, it was a dream, but it was not realistic. I was not prepared for all that life was about to throw at me

The life I was living was complex and I was only looking at it from one angle. The 1st time I had to navigate transition, I was 14 years old and in 9th grade. Suddenly, I was the only child at home, and what I knew as home life would change forever. I grew up in what society would say was an intact family. I had mom and dad at home, and they worked and provided for the children. So, the mention of my parents getting a divorce, and having to choose to live with one parent and not the other was devastating to me. I didn't know what I would do or what life would be like. My family dynamic as I knew it was over, and I had to learn to live in a single-parent house. My 9th grade year was one that will always stick in my head. Not only did I have to navigate being home alone with no siblings, but as a freshman in high school, I was navigating the loss of friendships and my parents fighting and arguing each day.

My mom eventually moved out the house. I watched my dad go through depression and I saw him try to navigate being a single parent with a daughter and having to navigate his own life situations. I remember many nights crying myself to sleep and waking up with puffy eyes. I was trying to find ways to hide the fact that I was going home to an empty house. My dad supported me in continuing my walk with God but at this point I was going to church out of habit. I would ask God why did you do this to me? Why did you allow my parents to break up? I was angry because I didn't understand why they couldn't hold off until I graduated. I blamed them and felt they were being selfish in making this decision and not considering how it would affect me. I had so many feelings and emotions and I didn't know how to deal with it. The few friends I had left at school would come to me and try to talk but I didn't have much to say. I didn't try out for basketball. I did band but I wasn't as happy because both of my parents were not at the games like it was before. It was no longer a big family thing for us to go to football games on Friday. What was normal became very unfamiliar to me.

My mom had moved out, and that's when I felt the void of my mom. Now, this was a very hard place for me. I went to all of the activities with a silent cry in me because I was missing the family dynamic that I had known all my life. During my high school years, I found myself making a lot of decisions based on my feelings about wanting to please people. I was led by my emotions in every area of my life. I created a life based on being accepted. I wanted someone to validate everything I did or accept me, or else I wouldn't do it. This became crippling to me. My 9th grade year was hard, and I am so happy I made it through. I finished the school year living with my dad, and then I would transition to Philadelphia to live with my mom. After all these years, all I saw was victory. I had never seen what seemed like defeat. I saw God pull my family through some tough times. I saw my mother pray and have faith and he showed up every time. In every battle in life, we often feel defeated and like God has forsaken or abandoned us, but He hasn't. He is with you, and because He is God, you are already victorious. I have heard the saying that you might lose the battle, but God always wins the **WAR**! So be encouraged to come out with victory, no matter what it looks like. You come out as **PURE GOLD**! You come out better than you went in. You might not notice it or see it until you have a moment of reflection, but the victory is there; it just may not look like victory. **WOW**!! Little did I know, I was victorious even in the middle of my life falling apart. I didn't break! I came out with my mind intact and moving towards building this new life. Now, some people may say that's no big deal, but as a young girl who had never lived without one of her parents, I didn't know how I would navigate life. I found myself in an identity crisis and in a low place. Depression found me, and that's when we began our relationship. I isolated myself from my friends because my home life was so chaotic. I didn't know what to do. I became a person pleaser, which cost me many things. This would have a domino effect on the issues that would later come into life.

I think we can all say that we have had some voids in life. We have tried to fill them with lots of other things. Sometimes, that can cause more damage than good. Well, here I was in high school with voids and didn't know how I would fill them, I didn't even know they existed. I just knew something was missing and I looked for all types of ways to gain that feeling of being complete and happy. So, I did what my peers told me made them feel complete and whole. I turned to sex and relationships. This is one of those things where I think of my parents old saying, *"if I would have known now what I knew then."* I was young, but I felt hurt and I needed something to fill it. And I knew I couldn't turn to drugs because I had been taught that no drug could fill your void. My parents had done all they could to keep me away from drugs and the street life, but they didn't talk to me about sex. I didn't know that opening myself up to sex would lead me down a road where it would become like a drug. I couldn't just get one hit. I had to keep going until I felt the feeling of relief and satisfaction. If you know anything about addiction, you know that you never get the satisfaction and relief you felt the first time. So, you will find yourself in a cycle trying to chase the first high. Not realizing that you are literally killing yourself. I know these things, but I didn't look at sex as an addiction. I didn't even see myself as being co-dependent in a relationship. Codependency is a dysfunctional relationship where one person assumes the role as the giver sacrificing their own needs and well-being for the sake of the other person. I was the giver. I wanted to please the person I was with and in this case, it was unhealthy because I was not honoring what I wanted. Making them happy was what I wanted even if that meant hurting myself. I did not know sex and co-dependency in a teenage girl is a recipe for disaster. I didn't talk to anyone, because I didn't want to feel judged, and I didn't have a space safe enough to be vulnerable. I thought having sex and being in a relationship was normal. All of my friends and people that I knew were doing it. So it couldn't be that bad. So, after months of feeling empty, I had to start school in a new state. It was rough. I found myself trying to find people to fit in with and eventually, I stumbled across a relationship with someone who excepted me. Not only did they accept me, but they were willing to invite me into their family. So, I found myself going over there after school. I was eating dinner with the family and going places with the family as if I was a part of the family. I loved it. It made me feel accepted and I needed that. So, whatever he wanted, I was willing to deliver because I felt love. My co-dependency kicked into full gear because I felt like I was being loved and he was always happy with what I did so it was great. Little did I know, my relationship would end. I started to notice when I spoke up about what I wanted, and I started to say no to certain things, our relationship would get rocky. That relationship eventually ended, and I found myself back on the market looking for a man to please and make happy.

This time I told myself I would stand up for myself a little more, but I didn't. I went right back to people pleasing and codependency. After years and years of feeling used and unheard I decided I was going to do something about it. If you know anything about cycles and patterns, they can be hard to break. You find yourself doing good for months then have a slip up and you go right back to what is familiar. I did this for years. In every relationship, I found myself filling voids and doing what was asked of me to feel accepted. I would have little to no boundaries. I would use my voice, but when it would yield a result. I didn't like entering back into a time of silence and pleasing people. My voice was being taken from me. The voice that I would need to advocate for myself. The voice I would need to decree and declare things. I didn't know that me not speaking up and standing on what I wanted would cause me to become silent and lose a part of my identity. I found myself more comfortable when I was quiet and didn't want the fight that came with having my voice. That was a tough time in life, and I gave up my voice and settled for silence to keep peace. At the end of high school, I had 3 relationships that shaped me into a person I didn't even recognize. When I looked in the mirror, I was a product of my environment. I was broken, barely holding on, in a silent depression and screaming for help in so many ways. I had friends and family around me but because I was so good at masking what was really happening, they didn't even know that I was self-medicating with sex and living a double life. I would go to church, volunteer, go to all the youth outings. I would pray, sing on the worship team and dance. No one knew that I was drowning on the inside. I had a relationship with God that was based on my mom. I didn't know God for myself. I allowed sex to be a god to me. It became my solution for everything. I found myself taking all of my problems to the bed instead of to God. I knew that it was getting bad, and I was praying but as much as I was praying, I was having sex. I just knew God was going to deliver me from my pain. So, I decided during my senior year, I was going to build a good life. It was senior year, and I was not going to shortchange myself because of what was happening in my life. I did almost every senior activity and I applied to all the schools I wanted to go to. My mind was made up that I would go to college and create this amazing life. I made a timeline for myself, and I knew God would let it happen just like I wanted as long as I worked hard at it. My plan was to get a bachelor's in accounting and then become a CPA. I would marry the man I met in college, and we would live in a high-rise in the downtown area of a major city. I would only have kids if he wanted children. I would travel all over. I had everything planned out and I was ready to put in the work. I had all these plans and God had some plans of his own. God answered my prayer to rescue me in an uncomfortable way. I got into my top school and got a scholarship. I was super excited. I got into an early admissions program and would have to go to school in July which was nice because I would be able to learn the campus and not feel as nervous when regular classes started. So, graduation came, and I was celebrating every day. Me and my friends were hanging and making our last weeks together, memorable. Well one day, about two weeks after high school graduation, I went to the hospital due to some bleeding and that day would change my life forever. I remember calling my best friend and asking her to go to the hospital with me. When we got there, I remember my parents calling back-to-back. This was very unusual because my parents didn't call me a lot at all. I kept ignoring the calls because I didn't know what was going on with my body. I wanted to wait to see how serious it was before I answered or told them anything. So, after some tests, the doctor came in the room with my results to see why I was bleeding and what he said took my breath away. He said, "Well CONGRATULATIONS Ms. Bacon you're going to have a baby." My eyes got wide, and they filled with tears. All I could think about was, how did I get here. This can't be real. He is playing a joke on me. This can't happen to me. I was going to church and doing everything everybody said. Why me? So many thoughts were going through my mind. Now, for some it would be the happiest day of their life. However, for an 18-year-old that had her whole life planned out, this news was devastating. The doctor not only told me that I was pregnant, but he didn't know if my baby was still alive or if my body was having a miscarriage because of the bleeding. So, they would need to run some more tests. At that moment, I looked at my best friend and said to call my mom. I didn't know how to handle this situation/I turned to the one person I knew would come through and help me figure out a solution. I just said mom, I am at the hospital. I need you to come here. Well, by the time she got to the hospital, the test results were in. The doctor came in to tell me, my baby was still alive, and it had a strong heartbeat. When he said that, my face looked like I had seen a ghost. My mom looked at me and said "What? Baby?"

He said, "Yes ma'am. She is 2 months pregnant." My mom's eyes looked at me with disappointment and tears. When he told me that he didn't know if it was alive, my hope was for it to be dead so that I could come out from underneath this horrible dream I was dreaming. So, I wouldn't have to tell anyone, and I could go on with life. However, the baby was alive and well, and I didn't know what to say. I didn't know what my mom would say, but I felt disappointment, condemnation, shame, and guilt at that moment. Those are some of the feelings that I would feel for years to come. I took those feelings, and, in my mind, I said because I have done this, I have to live with these feelings for life. They became a part of my identity. They became the things that would limit me in life. They would cause me to live underneath my means and settle for less than God's best for me. I would allow the birth of my son, which should be a blessing and joyous occasion, to become a place of pain. I began to feel like Naomi. I wanted to be called Mara meaning God has dealt harshly with me. That summer became incredibly stressful and dark. I found myself sick physically and mentally. I disconnected from church even the more because I was mad at God for letting this happen to me. I would distance myself from my friends because I didn't want them to ask me too many questions. For years to come, I would dim my light because of the shame of my past and allow myself to settle for whatever life had because I felt like I couldn't undo the wrong I had done. I would walk around like an orphan because

I didn't think I deserved the sonship of God because of my actions and deeds.

My prayer is that you don't allow your past to hold you back from your future. Yes, you did it and yes it happened, but God is sovereign. Not only that, He sent his son, Jesus, to die for our sin so, we didn't have to die, and we could live in freedom. I pray today that you will be able to embrace the freedom and love of Jesus Christ. Know that nothing can separate you from the Love of Jesus Christ. NOTHING! No baby out of wedlock, no abortions, no sin. NOTHING!

> [38] *For I am persuaded, that neither death, nor life, nor angels, nor principalities, nor powers, nor things present, nor things to come,*
>
> [39] *Nor height, nor depth, nor any other creature, shall be able to separate us from the love of God, which is in Christ Jesus our Lord.*
>
> **Romans 8:38-39**

After reading this section, think of the things you wrote in the previous sections.

How have you allowed those things to separate you from God's Sovereign love?

___

___

___

___

___

___

___

___

___

___

___

___

___

___

How have you given up on dreams that you had?

What is something in your life that has caused you to silence your voice?

Chapter Two

A LIFE I NEVER PLANNED

So there I was, lying in the hospital in complete disbelief of what was happening. I looked at my mom, and I saw disappointment in her eyes. At that moment, she had no words. We rode home in silence. When we got home, she told me that she had a plan. We would abort the baby and go on with life as normal. I would go to school, and everything would be fine. She made an appointment and told the child's father what they had to do to assist. Then, she called my siblings and told them what was happening. My brother came up to talk with me and my mom. After speaking with my brother and after many days of silence. I decided to take this journey of parenthood no matter how it looked. I was scared and nervous. I didn't know what was ahead of me, but I couldn't get rid of my baby. My parents were disappointed, but they were going to support me and help me as much as they could. So, in July, I went to school as planned, and I lived on campus... pregnant. My doctor told me that I would have to tell one person just in case of an emergency. I was fine with that. I told the one person who I was closest to. She didn't make me feel bad. She loved on me and always looked out for me. Now, I was at a very well-known Christian College. I knew I couldn't tell anyone because I didn't want to have to feel even more guilt and shame. At this point in my life, God began to reveal himself to me more. I began to ask God to speak to me and comfort me. I remember my college having Worship On The Hill. I would take me and my pregnant belly to the hill. We would sit and worship for hours. Just our voices and an acoustic guitar. I remember hearing God speak to me through my unborn son. I prayed that God would take care of me and my son. I didn't know how I would support a child with no degree and no job. As I lay in my bed, I heard God say to me, "I will take care of you." I remember the peace of God coming over me, and I began to cry. At that moment, I began to have an unexplainable amount of peace. From that day forward, God would begin to talk to me about how I had to experience certain things in life so I would be able to help others. Little did I know, having a baby out of wedlock was the first valley that God would walk through with me. The Bible says it like this. *And we know that all things work together for good to them that love God, to them who are the called according to his purpose.* (**Romans 8:28**). I didn't know that the darkness I had and would soon experience would help so many other people, but that was the first time I said Yes to God. I said, "Yes God! I will do what you want." I didn't know my "Yes" would cost so much. As I look back on it now, I am glad I said Yes.

So, I hid my pregnancy for 8 months. I went to classes. I did my work. I was active in college, and I made the most of it. My belly didn't show, and I would make sure I wore baggy clothes so that people wouldn't think anything. The closer I got to my due date, I would schedule my doctor's appointments around my class schedule. I would leave campus and ride the bus from one part of the city to another part of the city, just to see the doctor, and then return as if nothing happened. When it was time to register for classes for the next term, everybody was asking about my classes. In a heartbeat, I would change the topic. I felt like I wanted to run away because I didn't tell people why I hadn't registered for class.

Being in this Christian college, I knew that telling them that I was pregnant would not be good. However, I knew I couldn't keep avoiding the question. I told my RA that I wanted to make an announcement during weekly bible study. I told her what it was, and she just hugged me. She didn't judge me. She loved on me. It was shocking. She said, "sex is a sin, but the baby is a gift." This wasn't the first time I had heard this. My brother told me the same thing when he came to talk to me about being able to carry children, how God entrusted babies to people, and how it was an honor to be able to have a child. Tears filled my eyes as I felt the love of Jesus Christ overtake me. Even though I knew my baby was a gift, shame still crippled me, and I still had intrusive thoughts. However, I kept moving forward. She let me know that I would be missed and loved and that if I needed anything, to let them know. So, Wednesday came, and I told my hall that I would not be returning to school because I would be having a little boy in January. Some of them hugged me and congratulated me. Others crucified me and looked at me funny. It wasn't the first time that I would feel love and rejection at the same moment. The rejection hurt, but I knew that God loved me. That is what kept me. I knew it would happen, and I was ready for it. However, it still hurt. There is an old adage that says *sticks and stones may hurt my bones, but words would never hurt me.* Oftentimes, people don't really understand that words do hurt and they are seeds that are planted. If we don't uproot them fast, they can get watered and turn into grass, trees and other things.

I left school in December of 2008. I had every intention of coming back to school after one semester off. When I got home, my friends had a baby shower for me. I was overwhelmed with the love and support shared for me and my baby. I had so much stuff. It packed out my room. My mom had to create space for me to put stuff in the hall closet. God was showing me that He was going to take care of me. In January of 2009, I had a beautiful baby boy. He brought so much joy and happiness to my family. My family had a welcome home party where my baby boy was showered with even more gifts and words of wisdom from so many people. My family and friends surrounded me with so much love and support. Once again, I was completely overwhelmed.

I dealt with so much transition during that time. I went from being a high school graduate to a college student to now a full-time mom. I didn't navigate every transition well, but one thing I did do was keep my faith in God. I was confident that he would bring me out on the other side. I lost friendships because I secluded myself. I was so focused on being a mom. I put everything my son needed and wanted before myself. As a person who struggled with confidence, I parented my son so that he would be a reflection of me. I lost who I was because I did whatever he needed and wanted all the time to make sure he was happy. I didn't want my child to be taken from me because I was seen as a bad parent, so I was determined to be an overachieving parent. My dad had me scared that anything I did wrong would cause "someone" to take my baby. I knew that this would be a hard journey, but I didn't see any way out of this. I didn't know if I would even come out on the other side okay. I started to take it one day at a time. I had to sign up for welfare. I went to the Department of Social Services, and I told them that I needed help. I received food stamps, Medicaid, and WIC for me and my son. I would go to the grocery store at night so people wouldn't see me using my food stamps. I felt embarrassed and ashamed that I had to get the government to help me. I wanted to be self-sufficient, but I didn't see how that would happen. I can remember going to Save-A-Lot to get WIC items and not knowing how to use the check. The cashier had to show me what I could get and what I couldn't get. I was grateful for the program, but there was a level of shame that came with it. Yep! I had some pride issues. I was prideful and didn't like having to receive help. As a young parent, I knew that I needed to use these resources to help me and my child. However, I felt like a burden to others. I didn't want to become a statistic. Many people talked about how the welfare system could be a rat race and how people would be on it for generations and generations. I saw my parents work hard to get us out of housing and provide a good life for us. I knew that I wanted to do the same no matter what it took. There were many days and nights when I thought about how I could work hard and create a life for my kid without fully relying on the system.

As a new mom, I faced the same challenges as many new moms face. This included self-identity. I was trying to find myself. Who is Tanzania? Not only did I have to figure out who I was, but I also had to figure out how

I wanted to raise my son. I love how my parents raised me, but there were some things that I didn't want to bring into my parenting. I wanted to be a cool parent. I wanted my kids to always have what they wanted. Perfection is a far-fetched endgame that none of us will ever achieve. Parenting styles are specific to each child. This style isn't about the parent, but more about the child because they will all need different things.

The thought of school became a distant memory as my focus shifted to giving my son the world. I worked multiple jobs so I could provide the best life possible for my son. Then, in 2011, I found myself in love. Now, let me be honest. This came by surprise to me because I was in the streets living my best life. I didn't want a committed relationship, nor did I want to have any more children. Here's the most shocking thing. After dating this man for three months, I found out that I was with child. Talk about a pickle! I knew Tanzania! I knew what my situation was like. I wasn't fully committed to him, and he wasn't fully committed to me. We were playing around in what people would call a situationship. We decided to abort the baby because we didn't even know if we would be together in the next month or so.

I never thought that having an abortion would come with its own feelings of shame and guilt. Now, I was not only having kids out of wedlock, but I had aborted a child because I didn't want to deal with what I had done. I wanted a quick fix and no more responsibilities. He was happy because it kept us from full commitment. I was happy because I didn't want to be responsible for another mouth to feed. Lastly, I did not want to hear my dad's mouth. Having an abortion caused me to fall into another level of depression and shame. I couldn't talk to anybody about what I did because I didn't want to be judged. People would form an opinion about me, and I didn't want to deal with having to face people who viewed me as a baby killer. Yes! I aborted my baby, but I didn't do it because I had a cold heart. I did it for a ton of reasons that people wouldn't fully understand. I already had to deal with my own thoughts. I didn't have room for the opinions and words of other people. Many women have decided to abort children for various reasons. It is no one's job to judge them, but God. Our responsibility is to love them. In 1st Peter 4:8, it says, *"Above all, Love one another deeply, because love covers over a multitude of Sins"*. Did you read that? Love one another. We shouldn't judge people because at any point in life, you can be that person. Don't regret the decisions that you have made. You and God have to work it out together. It has taken me years to forgive myself and really come to a place of peace. I didn't do that by talking to people. I did it by going to therapy and having hard conversations with myself. I also prayed and talked to God, allowing Him to heal and speak to areas in my life that I didn't even know were affected by the abortion. This abortion would open the door to an abortive spirit. For years, I would abort many things in life, and I'm not talking about babies. I aborted dreams. I aborted visions. I aborted vision, business ideas, and goals. I found myself in a revolving cycle of starting things and never finishing them. This cycle would be on repeat for years and years.

After the abortion, me and my love continued our situationship, and it got crazy. We dealt with drama from outside people as well as issues with the law. Maybe we did want to be with each other. After my birthday, we decided to move to the south to build a better life for our kids. My partner had been in the streets and wanted to start a new life, and I was in full support of it. We planned to move right after

Valentine's Day in 2011. By that time, we would have been talking for about eight months. We agreed to become an exclusive couple when we moved. We moved to North Carolina as planned but what came next was a total shock to me. Yes! Another shock!

After living in North Carolina for about two weeks, my partner told me that he could not deal with the slow-paced life in the South and that he would be going back to Philadelphia. I didn't understand why he wanted to go back to a place that he wanted to leave so badly. I didn't understand what people meant when they said that the streets would grip you and not let you go. My parents worked so hard to keep me away from the streets, and I basically signed a love contract with it. My partner went back to Philadelphia, and we said that we would continue our relationship. I began to become somebody I didn't know. I started lying more, being secretive, and allowing things to happen that I never allowed before. I fell in love with a man who loved the streets. On top of that, I fell in love with what he, the life, and the streets provided for us. Remember how other situations came with shame and guilt? This life came with instability, but I was doing what I knew to do.

I was doing whatever the person I love wanted me to do.

    This led me down a road that would cause me to put me and my kids in situations that would jeopardize our well-being and safety. I made decisions that could have changed our lives forever because I was so hungry for love and affection. We had a good life, and we were raising our children. I just knew that we would be together forever and that I had found what I had been longing for. I wanted the two-parent household for my kids like that I had most of my life. I wanted them to enjoy vacations. I wanted them to have daddy days with their dad. I wanted daughter days with the girls. We began to create the life we wanted, but we were coming from two different worlds. He was a street dude, and I was a good girl who came up in the church and lived a very sheltered life until high school. Even though we lived in two different states, it was actually working. We were building a life together and I was grateful for that. In October of 2011, I found out I was carrying another baby and to my surprise, my partner wanted us to keep the baby. So, even though I was still not convinced that I wanted another child, I was going to keep the baby to please my partner. The pregnancy was going well until my partner demanded that we no longer live in two separate states. It costs a lot of money to run back and forth from NC to Philly to be with each other. So, I decided, at eight months pregnant, I would quit my job and move back to Philadelphia to be with him. Our family would be complete and we would raise the kids and live happily ever after.

> **Full Disclosure:**
>
> **I am a girl who likes to live in a fantasy world sometimes. I was always picturing the perfect ending that would lead to a happily ever after picture-perfect family. What does that look like? I really don't know. I was just looking to be happy and whole.**

I moved to Philadelphia, and we began to develop this life. We had an efficiency apartment, a car, and each other. That's all we needed. We started running the streets again. It looked promising and fruitful. I was excited to be back with my friends and enjoying the city life. I delivered a healthy baby boy, and now I felt like my world was complete. I had my two children, my man, and a life that I would have planned. My dad would always tell me to be careful what I was doing and to take care of myself. I didn't tell him what we were doing, and he didn't ask too many questions. He just told me to be careful and to keep me and the boys safe. My partner had big dreams about our life. I was okay with them, but I was nervous.

One day, he came up with a big plan and he simply said to me, "Don't worry. We gone be good." So, I believed him. I had just started a new job. Me and my friend wanted to go out to celebrate. I wanted to do karaoke. We went to do karaoke and it was amazing. I didn't know that going to karaoke would save my life. My partner's big plan would lead us to have a run-in with the law where I would be facing prison time. The person I loved put my name on paperwork that would send me to prison. I was terrified. How could love lead me down this road? A road where I would have to choose either me or the man I loved. I didn't want to have to choose. I wanted to be able to have my cake and eat it too. I thought that love could do no evil. I thought love would cover me. So here I was standing in the middle of choosing if I loved myself more than I loved him. I didn't know what I would do.

On April 23rd, 2014, I received the unselfish, unconditional love of Jesus Christ. It was a divine setup. I had been praying for God to save me. As I was walking to my father's house to get my mail, God sent a divine interruption for me. I saw a man sitting in front of the house, but I didn't pay him too much attention. Here's the thing. He knew who I was.

He exited the car and said, "Ms. Bacon?"

I said, "Umm.... Yes?", with a puzzled look on my face.

He said, "I am the detective you've been dodging."

I said, "Oh goodness!"

He told me to just be calm and he talked to me, ensuring me that he wanted to hear me out. I knew street code and didn't want to break it however, I didn't want to live by the streets anymore. I am grateful that God always covers us. He told me that they had evidence that I didn't do what was done and that I would not be charged. He showed me my whole life. He knew who my parents were, where they worked, and where I had attended school. He told me everything that he knew about me and how I got caught up in something that I really didn't know about. He encouraged me to turn my life around. I guaranteed him that I would. That was God giving me a second chance at life. That was God showing up for me when I couldn't show up for myself. That was a God-moment.

For weeks, I had been trying to figure out how to get out of it. I didn't want to deal with it. I wanted to wake up and it was gone. That day when I got home, I booked a ticket to North Carolina, and I said I was going home. Philadelphia is the home of my birth, but North Carolina is the place where I was raised, and I learned so much about life. I knew that I had to go back so I could get my footing and live a better life for myself and my kids. So, I packed my two duffle bags and my kids' car seats, and I got on a train to return to North Carolina. I felt like the prodigal son. I had gone to the big city and wasted all of my inheritance and all that I had. When it got bad, I went back home with nothing. When I got there, God welcomed me with open arms. I felt like I had escaped. I didn't realize that this was an answered prayer from when I asked God to get me out. And that's exactly what He did!

Did you know that love comes with soul ties? Man! I was yoked up. My prayer life was fervent and fulfilling. I just didn't like how God was answering them. Oftentimes, we pray to God expecting an answer, but when He delivers, we become clueless as to what is happening. There are times when I have to remind myself. Tanzy – You prayed for this! I didn't know that God was setting me free from bondage. By moving, I no longer had to live that life. I entangled myself in it, but He came and set me free. I begged my partner to come with me to live the better life that we dreamed and talked about. He said he would come when the time was right.

There I was, in North Carolina, with my 5-year-old, and my 1-year-old, less than 500 dollars to my name, no car, and no job. I had nothing. I didn't know what I was doing but I knew the life we were living had caught up to me and I couldn't do it anymore. I was done with the street life. I wanted more out of life and for my life. I was convinced that I didn't want to live like that anymore. Have you ever wanted something that was better for you, but you didn't know how to get to it? It's like wanting greatness, but mediocrity has you in a chokehold. I was in deep. All I knew to do was work and take care of my kids. All of this was a divine interruption caused by God. God saved me! He didn't just save me from jail time, but he saved me from myself. He didn't allow anything to follow me. I was able to come to North Carolina with a clear conscious and clean record. I was determined to come back and make things right for my children. I worked hard. I took a 3rd shift job at a warehouse making very little, but I was determined not to stop. I looked for jobs during the day and took care of my kids. I went to the social services office to get food stamps and Medicaid. I used my sister's car to go to work. I walked to take care of errands. Did I say that I was determined? I did not allow my limitations to hold me back. I applied to jobs I wasn't even qualified for. It started with a 3rd shift job in a warehouse. Then, I started working 3rd shift in a group home. I loved it, but I needed more money. I applied for the United States Postal Service. After 2 months, they finally called me back. I started that job in November of 2014.

Before I started my new job, I saved enough money to buy my first car and get my first apartment. That was a big accomplishment for me. It was my first step towards self-sufficiency. As the baby of my siblings, I also looked at them to measure where I should have been. I was 24. I had two children. I finally had a job and a car. I felt like a failure when I looked at them, but I always kept looking at them to motivate me to do more. I was proud to get out of the situation, but I knew I wanted more. As long as I kept working hard, I would get more.

You're going to think I'm crazy, but I wanted my partner to come back to North Carolina. Don't forget. Soul ties are real, and love will have you out here doing some crazy things. I knew that my partner still wanted to be a part of the streets, but I was determined to change him. He eventually came to North Carolina. We were working, taking care of our kids, and building a better future for them. We were finally starting to live out what we had talked about many nights. Working, taking care of the kids, building a better for them. No illegal activities. Just honest work and living a wonderful life. I thought we were happy until one day, I saw him texting someone, and I didn't understand how that could be. He was with me but still longing to be in the city. He was being pulled between two different worlds.

I didn't think anything could happen to make him go back but the streets had a mean grip on him. And when it hooks you? It's like good bait to a fish. When it's good, you swallow the whole hook, and that's when it becomes detrimental to you.

I grew up in a program called Narcotics Anonymous. In that program, it tells us that the streets will lead us to bitter ends: jails, institutions, or death unless we find a new way to live. I was trying to help the man who I loved to find a new way to live. I dedicated my life to showing him a different way that would bring us so much happiness, but it was like I was fighting a never-ending battle. The streets have a way of making things that are not good for us look good to us. It tries to pull us back and makes us feel bad when we don't want to indulge.

In January of 2015, my love decided that he couldn't live the southern way anymore. He decided to go back to Philadelphia and my heart was crushed. The man I wanted to be with forever was leaving and I didn't know what to do. He chose the streets over living a better life. I was angry, sad, hurt, and disappointed. He wanted to be a good man, but it was hard for him to push through and learn to do that in a way where the streets didn't play apart. He knew how to navigate the streets, and he knew who he was, but he didn't know who he was outside the streets. Living in a foreign place like North Carolina was hard for him. He didn't see himself fitting in. He couldn't see himself as the man he was for me without the streets. Oftentimes, we become the very thing we are doing, and we don't know who we are once we are out of it. This was the first real relationship I had in my adult life, and I had given so much to it. I just knew that I would get my happily ever after. I prayed that God would save him and open his eyes to come back to North Carolina. I made many promises to God. If He answered me, I would do so much. I was starting to go back to church even though I still wasn't all the way sold on it. My partner and I decided that he would return to Philadelphia, and we would co-parent, and then, he would eventually come back.

Chapter Three

BROKEN FOR THE SAKE OF BEING BUILT

On July 28th, 2015, my love was murdered. The life we talked about would never come to pass. Not only was my heart shattered, but my life was shattered. I didn't want to live. How would I raise my kids as a single parent? How would I maintain? Why would God do this to me? Why would he allow it to happen? I had so many questions and so many emotions. I didn't know how to express it. I couldn't understand why a God who could raise people from the dead, allow my love to die. When he died, a part of me died too. I couldn't understand why God would hurt me so badly. I felt as if God didn't like me. My head was hurting. My heart was physically hurting, and I couldn't think straight. I kept replaying the conversation we had had for about 2 hours before he died. We talked about him coming back to North Carolina and what would be different.

His phone was about to die, and I was getting ready to get off work. I told him to call me when his phone was charged and he promised that he would. He said, "I love you big head" and I said, "I love you too." About 20 minutes later, while going through our nightly closing procedures, I received a phone call asking me to call him because he wasn't answering his phone. I began to call him and my heart began to sink. My friend said, "Tanz, he is dead."

I don't remember much after that. I cried the whole way home. I couldn't talk. I told my sister that something happened, and he wasn't here anymore. My eyes were red, and I became numb. I couldn't feel anything. I didn't understand why. The doctors called it a state of shock. Remember the song and movie "Thin Line Between Love and Hate? Well, I was walking a thin line between sanity and insanity. I fabricated different scenarios in my head about what was going on. All of the scenarios were created in an effort to convince myself that this was a sick joke that he was playing. In my mind, at some point, he would call and tell me that he was okay. I didn't believe it was real until I saw his body. Even then, my brain was trying to get me to think that it was all a cover-up. I didn't know how I would go on. Honestly, I didn't want to go on.

I was in a dark place, not understanding why God or anybody would do this to me. It wasn't done to just me. It was done to my children too. Why would life show up for me like this? I questioned God, people, and even myself. My words were very limited. I didn't want to talk: to people or to God. I didn't want people praying for me. I prayed so much the night it happened that when I arrived in Philly, and he was not alive, I really questioned God. I didn't want to hear anything about belief, faith, prayer, or God. I was angry with God. I blamed him. I felt like Martha and Mary when their brother Lazarus died. I didn't understand why God didn't run to my rescue when I called him. I did what He asked of me. I was living for Him as best I could, and He still allowed the man who loved me to die. At this point in life, I was so confused, I just didn't understand why a loving God would want to see me so hurt. It was like every time I took a step forward, I got knocked 10 million steps back. I blamed everyone because I felt like no one wanted me to prosper or succeed, and this relationship would have proven the people wrong.

As I rode from North Carolina to Philadelphia, I just gazed out the window the whole ride. This was a ride that I had taken so many times that it had become short for me. This time, the ride was the longest and darkest ride that I had ever taken. I cried so much, that my eye ducts were hurting. I felt like I wouldn't have any more tears in me. I stayed in Philadelphia for 5 days and every night I would stay up and cry. The only word that I could get out was JESUS. At night, I would hold myself and rock back and forth saying," Jesus, Jesus, Jesus." I felt my mind slipping away from me. I began to think thoughts that were not good and then I would say, "Jesus." During one of the hardest times in my life, I was angry with God – the only person that could fix it. What do you do when you're in a season and angry with God, yet you find solace only in reaching out to Him? What's the response that you give? For me, saying His name brought a peace that I knew I needed. I couldn't understand why such a loving and sovereign God could want to see me so hurt and broken. Oddly enough, the potter was breaking me to put me back together. I didn't want to be broken. I didn't ask to be broken, but God saw fit to break me so He could build me back up.

To be honest, that season of my life should have killed me. I had so many suicidal thoughts and some homicidal ones as well. I wanted revenge for what had been done, and I wanted someone to suffer as much as me. I didn't want the law to be involved. I wanted to take justice into my own hands. I was a walking robot. I remember going to work every day and barely being able to work. I would run to the bathroom, cry for about 15 minutes, and then go back to work. I would come home from work, feed the kids, watch movies, and then I would put a little something in my cup so I could sleep at night. First, it was a little something to sleep at night. Then, it was a little something to get me going in the morning. I was drowning in broad daylight, but nobody knew it. I suffered in silence. Not using my voice caused me to sink deeper and deeper into depression. I was going through life making sure to check all of the boxes, but I wasn't connecting with anything. I worked so much, that my family and friends were raising my babies. I was just financially providing for them. I shut everything out. Sex and alcohol became my coping mechanisms. I wanted to die. Once again, I questioned God. Why do you have me here? My kids were my only reason for living. However, I am grateful that in a season where I didn't know what to say or do, God covered me. I continued walking the line of sanity and insanity as my mental, physical, and spiritual health were challenged. Thanks to God I didn't tip over on the side of insanity. I fought every night. I spent many nights crying out to God, yelling at Him, and telling Him my feelings. Then, I cried myself to sleep only to wake up to the same pain and grief. This cycle repeated for a long time.

> **Tanzy's Thought:**
>
> **God can handle all your emotions, feelings, hand gestures, and tantrums. He is well-equipped to deal with it. He made you, so he knows what you're feeling.**

I hear you! If he knows my feelings, why do I have to tell Him? I'm so glad you asked. You need to tell Him to give them back to Him. God wants us to come to Him vulnerable and open to give it all back to Him so He can handle it. He is a gentleman. He wants to handle you with care, but He wants you to bring it to Him to handle. Whatever you're going through, take it right to God. The one who has written the story.

Here's how it will play out.

As you continue to give it to Him, one day you will wake up and realize, "WOW! I didn't cry myself to sleep last night!"

Then, the next day you will be like, "Wow! I went a whole day and I was happy with joy."

Months later, you will find yourself wearing clothes in colors other than black.

After some years pass, you will remember the person that you lost on that special day and not cry all day.

I am not saying it will happen overnight, but I will say this. It will not always be like this. Rome was not built in a day. God will allow you to come out on the other side. You may still grieve, but you're not grieving like you were before. We grieve all the time in life. Grieving is a part of transition and life. People often ask me how I do it. My answer will always and forever be - God did it for me. God caused my love to die, and it caused me to reconnect to God in a new way. His death brought me to my knees. When I look back, all I can say is God carried me through. He didn't allow me to be consumed. He was with me. Every day, I would get up, get dressed, and do life. Like clockwork, I showed up for everybody, and I did everything. At night, I would drink just to go to sleep. This caused me to return to my old cycles. I began to rehearse the narratives that were in my head. This included word curses that I had come into agreement with. My mind began to tell me that I wouldn't find anybody who loved me like that. Who would want me? I have two kids with different fathers out of wedlock. These lies fueled my cycles and made me feel like I was right for doing what I did because I wasn't worthy of true, genuine, pure love. I was never going to get it. Giving myself to whoever I wanted was something I did to self-satisfy. I found myself in a place of settling for whatever life gave me. I had given up on trying to do things right. I was gone get it however I needed to.

Let me pause here for a minute. For many years I tried to create and navigate my own life without considering God. At this point in my life, I was at a crossroads. I had to decide if I was going to continue making attempts to create my own narrative or if I was going to allow God to create my story. I am a firm believer that God will bring us to different crossroads in our lives so we can decide to choose Him. It's called a place of surrender. Oftentimes, I find myself back at this place, where I am giving God all of me and saying use me for His glory. Now listen. Sometimes, we don't do it right on the first go-round. Then, there are times when you run for years and years like I did. God has a way of bringing things full circle. It's almost like a hamster in the hamster wheel or a dog that chases its tail. After seeing that same thing year after year, you are bound to get tired. The thing I love about God is that He is patient with us, and he suffers long with us. He doesn't give up on us after the first time. He sticks with us. Choosing God comes with a level of maturity. The seasoned folks always say, "Girl, you gone get sick and tired of being sick and tired." And I believe when you come to the end of your rope, that's when God can really work. Sadly, sometimes, we must get to the end of ourselves. However, I am grateful that when we come to the end of ourselves, we have a God who has no end, and He allows His strength to be perfected through us. I am grateful that God doesn't give up on us. Scripture says it like this in Psalm 86:15 (ESV): *"But you, O Lord, are a God merciful and gracious, slow to anger and abounding in steadfast love and faithfulness."* I am grateful that He is merciful and gracious and always abounds in love. He is a God who suffers long with us. He doesn't give up on us. Can you just pause for a moment and thank God for never giving up on you?

After months and months of being in a dark place, and just going through life, and allowing life situations to happen, I found myself making decisions from a place of grief. I didn't have a sound mind and my vision was blurry. I just knew I wasn't going to let 2016 go out without me gaining control over my life again. I found myself looking for love and answers in so many places. The song says, *"looking for love love in all the wrong places."*

I started a friendship with a friend's brother. After four months of talking, we decided to get married. I know. I know. I know exactly what you are wondering. What was I thinking? That's the thing. I wasn't thinking. I knew what I wanted and I was on the hunt for someone who was willing to do what I wanted so I could make it happen. I spent 2 months going back and forth between the prison and my marriage. I remember when I finally got the approval that I could get married. I drove to Peterburg, Virginia to get my marriage license and I was so excited. My soon-to-be husband called me because he had just been told that we got the approval. We talked for 15 minutes and then I went into the courthouse and got the paperwork. I had the rings, the paperwork, and now I was ready to be MRS. I didn't want anyone to know. I figured once we had all the ducks aligned, I would tell my family and friends. I was having a cookout on that Saturday and I said what a perfect time to tell everyone. I remember everybody coming over on the day of the cookout and we were all outside talking and joking. I said, "I have something to tell you all and they were like what?" Being the jokester in my family. I loved a good joke. I said, "I am getting married next week."

Everybody laughed. They said, "Yeah right. We know you. You're not getting married."

I tried to convince them that I was. They wanted to meet him and I said, "Well, you can't because he is in prison." Then I started to get the serious looks. Everyone began to tell me about how it was a bad idea and I really needed to rethink everything. Nobody wanted me to get married. Not only was he in prison, but he was in another state. None of that mattered to me because I felt this was the first time I was truly happy. I didn't understand why they didn't want to see me happy. From what I could tell about myself, I was happy with it. I wanted to be loved, but I also wanted to be in control. Everyone was getting married, being in relationships, and living life. I was just existing. I wanted to live like everyone else. I remember my sister and her best friend taking me to dinner and trying to have an intervention with me. They tried to convince me that I wasn't making a wise decision with sound judgment due to still dealing with the grief of losing my love, who died less than a year prior. They begged me to not go through with this plan. They said if you all really love each other, you can wait. I didn't want to wait. So, I went against everything everyone said. At this point in my life, I was blind. I couldn't see clearly, and I had people around me who could. I didn't want them to tell me anything other than what I wanted to hear.

I didn't understand the importance of community. It is imperative to have people around you who will hold you accountable. You need people who can see what you can't see. These are the same people who can help you navigate through life. I had community but I refused to embrace them. I wanted to be in control. So, in October of 2016, I got married. I didn't give any second thoughts or consideration to anything. I wanted to feel what I wanted to feel in that moment. In life, we get in spaces where we make life-changing decisions without a sober mind. In the Bible, it talks about counting the costs. I didn't count the costs. I just wanted to be happy in the moment and I did just that. As you're reading this, I'm sure you're wondering how I could even in the right state of mind to do that. Well, guess what? I wasn't, but I did it anyway. How many times have we tried to control a situation and made it worse because we couldn't see past the first layer? I created a false narrative and being to live in this fantasy world that would soon come crashing down.

God is so AMAZING! He saves us from the enemy and other people. He also saves us from ourselves. He doesn't allow us to mess up what he has for us. I got married. I was living life, doing what I wanted to do, and being in control of my own story again until life showed up, and I was faced with another crossroad. After about 8-9 months, me and my husband began to have major problems in our marriage. I didn't know what to do. I was giving my all mentally, financially, and emotionally. I was traveling to prison to see him every weekend that

I could. I was being supportive and encouraging through every obstacle. However, we had hit a rough patch, and we didn't know what to do. I reached out to my Pastors who were supportive and willing to help us navigate and work through it. However, we were not willing to make it work. We couldn't see what the other one was saying and we argued with each other, never coming to a better place. I decided that I didn't want to be in a marriage that always had issues. I filed for a divorce. I had to get myself out of this. It can't be that hard to just file for a divorce, and it be over. I did my research. Since we had no kids together and had never physically lived together, I could get a divorce quickly.

Now, let's talk about the goodness of God and how, even in our decisions, He will only allow us to go but so far before He guides us right back to the path, He needs us on. I was headed to divorce court, and even then, I had a ton of feelings. After years of trauma and disappointment, I found myself numbing my feelings of pain because I didn't want to deal with it, nor did I want to address it.

Here is another plug. Therapy is good. I will always be a BIG ADVOCATE of God and therapy. God delivers us and always will. We also need to go to therapy and learn some tools to help us stay delivered. Therapy doesn't take the power away from God. So, let me suggest that as you go through transition periods and times, seek counseling. Not just spiritual counseling but also counseling that will help us heal and unlearn some behaviors and patterns that we have created. We can come out of the situations and still have some residue on us because our souls have taken a hit. Therapy allows us to take care of our soul. It allows us to pick up the pieces, heal, and rebuild with a healthy foundation.

I tried to correct my life. I got to court to get my divorce. I had to sit there and wait my turn. As I waited, I said, "God, please get me out of this situation." Now, I prayed this prayer before, and less than three days later, he got me out of the situation. So, I just knew he would get me out of this one too. Why is it that we get ourselves in situations that we never asked God about from jump? Then, we expect Him to just get us out immediately. I wanted God to come in like He did before and deliver me quickly. LOL! Well, it wasn't going to be that easy. They called my case up to be heard and I remember the judge greeting me and then saying, "You're here for a divorce?"

I said, "Yes Sir."

He looked at me and read over the information quickly. I didn't expect to hear what would come out of his mouth next. The Judge said, "Well, that was a dumb decision to marry someone who was incarcerated. And now you think that I am going give you an easy way out.?"

I said, "Yes, sir. I know it was not the best choice."

He said, "Yea. Well, I am dismissing the case, and I am not going to rule on this. Get a lawyer and come back."

My eyes filled with tears. I was mad. Why didn't he just grant the divorce? Now, I was going to have to get a lawyer and pay money that I didn't have to get this done. I was so disappointed because he had the power to do what I needed him to do, but he wouldn't because he didn't want to. I couldn't understand why he wouldn't help me get out of this marriage. So, after feeling defeated, I said I was going to get a lawyer and do whatever I needed to do to get this divorce.

After almost a year of back and forth with the courts and my husband, my divorce was final on April 1st,

2018. I was finally awarded my divorce, and I was excited because, once again, God rescued me. It was a time of celebration, and I couldn't be happier even though I was officially single again. I had just gone through what I would say was the valley of the shadow of death. I was in a low place during my divorce and that's when I began to really come into a relationship with God for myself. I had been in therapy, and I started to pull back the layers of my life and deal with some hard things. I began to see my limiting beliefs show up in my actions and my words. I knew that I couldn't continue like this. I told myself that I would focus on myself and my children. I would dive deeper into my relationship with God. Sometimes in life, we must be honest and say it's not the devil or other people. We must realize that we are the problem. We put ourselves in situations that cause us to not have good outcomes. We make decisions that put us in a situation, and then we want out when it's not what we think. God can save us from any situation, but sometimes, God allows us to sit in situations so that we can learn some lessons. Not just that – sometimes, we want to skip the process and get straight to the reward. However, the process allows us to be prepared to fully handle the rewards. We must be more intentional and honest with ourselves when making decisions.

After being divorced and going through that process, I found myself in a place where I wanted God to really work on me. I wanted to be better. I found myself in some bad situations, and I was grateful that God had gotten me out. However, I knew I needed to grow up and embrace maturity in another way. I had to get honest with myself about where I was and where I wanted to go.

My kids have always been one of the things that kept me grounded and on the straight and narrow. However, I had to decide that I wanted to make a better decision for myself. As I went through my divorce process at the end, I realized my kids were in a bad situation. I had lost sight of being a good parent and giving them a good life. My kids were not being taken care of mentally, and emotionally like they should have been. I had to change that. My son got into some trouble at school, and they wanted me to attend parenting classes to help me be a better parent. I was insulted and hurt. I did not fully understand why they would suggest this, but I signed up and went. It was a 14-week class that I would have to attend. They said we would learn how to be better parents and could bring a support person. The perks were that we got some coins at the end, they fed us dinner, and they provided childcare. I was like, I could do this. It will be worth it in the end. So, I grabbed my support person and started on this journey.

At first, I did it because I had to, but around week 5, I started making connections and really getting to know people, and I opened myself up to learn parenting through a different lens. We did a bunch of role-play activities. It began to challenge me in my thinking and in my beliefs. The class allowed me to write about my own parenting journey and what I wanted it to look like. No one person is a perfect parent. However, we all can be good parents if we are intentional about how we do it. Don't ever allow anyone to tell you that you're not parenting well. It may not be the way they do it; what works for one parent may not work for another, and what works for one child may not work for the other. Be confident, knowing that you are doing the best thing for you and your children. Parenting is a journey, and it is full of ups and downs, and surprises and defeats, but the end is amazing. My world felt like it was falling apart, but in the same way, it felt like it was falling together.

Something was happening between me and my kids, and it was something beautiful. I didn't fully understand what it was. After a failed marriage and being summoned to a parenting class, I completed the course, and my life changed. I gained friendships. I gained insight that I would not have been able to do had I not started talking **to** my children and not **at** my children. I started looking at my kids and asking myself what impact I wanted to have on this earth. What do I want people to know me and my children by?

In the next couple of years, I began this journey of WHOLENESS for me, and my kids. We were all in therapy. I began to embrace my village and how it looked. I started to live in my truth while extending grace to myself so I could begin to live. I formulated new morals and values that I wanted me and my kids to live by. I began to seek out not just friendships but healthy friendships, as well as a mentor. I needed someone who I could be fully transparent with and who could help me navigate this new life. When you begin a journey to self-discovery, you notice how many unhealthy patterns and cycles you have. I stopped turning to sex for the answer. I purchased a Bible, and I began to read it for myself. SO! When I removed sex from my coping mechanism, I had to think of healthy coping skills. This is where I found my love for praying. I remember many nights wanting to turn to sex for my answer and instead, I would just begin to have a conversation with God. I would walk back and forth in my apartment and just tell God all that I was feeling, and I would say, "Holy Spirit come on in and sit with me." I would cry out and He would always come sit with me. My hunger increased for good things in my life and even more for the things of God in my life.

I told God that I was getting frustrated with some things, and I needed an answer. I had never gone to a church different from my family. I was always a tag along and I was okay with that. In this journey of self-discovery, I found out that I was a natural-born leader. Over the years, I allowed things to suppress my leadership abilities because I wanted to fit in. I talked to my mentor about churches and what I wanted in a church. She encouraged me to write a list of the things I wanted and to pray for them. I agreed to make the list, but I didn't want to go to a new church. I wanted God to fix where I was so I could just stay in a place of comfortability. After all, this is not a life I dreamed of or a life I even thought I would be successful at. I was a good girl turned bad girl, and turned back to a good girl. I just wanted to live a good life, have an active relationship with Jesus, and raise my kids. I trusted her, made the list, and began praying.

As I began praying, God started working. In February of 2019, I visited a church. I had seen a post from someone I knew when I was a kid. I saw what the church was doing, and I wanted to visit. No one would know me and because it had been over 15 years since I saw that person, I didn't think they would recognize me. After going through my divorce and parenting classes, my kids and I had a hard conversation about how they didn't always trust my judgment. I knew that visiting a new church would be hard for them. However, we went to the church. They asked so many questions, and I embraced them all. We had a great time at church. I remember wanting to sit in the back of the church, get what I need, and leave. To my surprise, they had a seat, but it was close to the front, and so the greeter walked me to the seat. I immersed myself in the worship experience. Before I knew it, the pastor called me out to speak a word to me. I'm not the spotlight type of person and I don't like to be called out. God really listens to me. Everything the Pastor said to me was on point. I visited the church for a few months. My initial prayer was that God would do a work in the place I was. However, I was still praying for the church that was on this list. After about five months, I heard God tell me to join this church. I didn't want to do it. I gave God my list of reasons.

1. They don't have everything from my list. As a matter of fact, they don't many of anything from my list.
2. It was filled with college students and people who were young and living a surrendered life.
3. I wanted to stay where I was comfortable.

For once in my life, I was beginning to find stability and my kids and I were thriving. I didn't want to disrupt what was happening. I struggled for about three weeks with the decision. Finally, I joined this church. From that day forward, my life would change. While in prayer, God told me that this wasn't just for me, but it was for my entire family. My family was in such a bad place. My mom brought us up in church and we knew the way, but we were all doing our own things. I didn't know how God was going to do it, but I was in agreement with it all. I was closing out 2019 with a bang and I loved it. Even though I transitioned churches, I was happy and everything seemed to be working out.

During my transition, some relationships were lost and I had to learn how to grieve relationships that I thought would be in my life for a lifetime. People who had been there with me at my worst barely answered my calls. I didn't know how to deal with it. This is what I did know. When I prayed, God would hear me. I stopped talking about a lot and I started to pray about everything. My family turned back to God. My kids embraced our new church family. I worked through my insecurities. In my attempt to embrace community, I looked to my church members for encouragement.

In 2020, I returned to school. As soon as I started to come out of my shell, the world shut down. I did not fully understand what was happening, but I knew I had to trust God. I made the hard decision to not work so I could stay home and support my kids. I remember asking God what was I going to do. As I prayed, God reminded me that in 2008, he made me a promise that he would always take care of me and my kids. I put all of my trust in God. My kids were surrounded by support from school. People were dropping off clothes, food, and all types of things that we needed. This is where I learned the importance of a village and how together, we could do anything. The pandemic was one of the hardest things to deal with mentally, physically, and financially. However, with God and my village, me and my children never lacked anything. I am grateful that during that time I was able to move into a bigger home, go on trips, and build lasting memories with my kids.

I continue to grow in my faith and God continues to answer prayers that I forgot I prayed. We lost so many people during the pandemic and some people lost themselves. I am grateful that during that time, I found who I was and what I stand for. I got my voice back. I broke cycles and patterns that I had held onto for years. I learned how to pivot in my parenting and grow under pressure. I didn't know who I was becoming, but my prayer to God was, "not my will, but thy will be done." I was praying a dangerous but amazing prayer. I was asking God to transform me into who He called me to be and to allow me to let go of my will and embrace His will. My old desires became things that I would hesitate to do. My appetite changed. I found myself speaking out and bringing my thoughts subject to Jesus. It was scary because I didn't know who I would become but I knew it would be who God created me to be. I started to have an identity crisis because I no longer identified with my sin but with my Savior. I found myself living a life I could have never imagined for me and my kids.

Here's a harsh reality. I never saw myself living past July 28th, 2015. I didn't have a desire for life. But here we are! It was 2022, and I was living a great life. Now I didn't have everything I wanted but I had my right mind, a relationship with God, and my kids. That's all I needed. This is a good place in my Wholeness Journey and I am proud.

So many times, in this season of my life I would ask God where are you? I sometimes would ask do you hear me? In this season I learned that God's will was not always convenient but it was protection and peace in his will. My question to you is whether you are in his will or your will? Are you trying to manipulate his hand or are you surrendering to the process? Not just surrendering to the process but are you following the instructions no matter what they seem like?

_____
_____
_____
_____
_____
_____
_____
_____
_____
_____
_____
_____
_____

Chapter Four

THE WELL OF REDEMPTION

As I reflect on my journey, I am reminded of the powerful encounter between Jesus and the Samaritan woman at the well. In that sacred moment, Jesus met her with grace and truth, revealing everything about her life without a hint of judgment. Like her, I have faced my own struggles and have wandered through the complexities of life, yearning for understanding and acceptance. God, in His infinite love, spoke to me in those quiet moments, addressing the parts of me that had been longing for years. I didn't always know what I was searching for, but as He gently revealed His love, I began to find true satisfaction in His presence. Throughout my life, I have navigated numerous transitions and made decisions that led me away from God and the church. However, each of those experiences brought me back to Him, teaching me invaluable lessons along the way. I have earned my Bachelor's degree in Psychology. I am building an agency dedicated to supporting families, and I embarked on my Master's degree journey. I have secured fulfilling positions within local government, all while watching my children thrive in the arts and sports. These accomplishments stand as testaments to the resilience and growth that can arise from a life lived in pursuit of purpose. Yet, I must acknowledge that my life is not perfect. I still grapple with battles and sometimes find myself falling back into old patterns. However, I have learned that it's not about never stumbling; it's about how quickly I choose to rise again. The journey is not defined by our mistakes but by our ability to recognize that no failure can keep us from the promises and life that God has already planned for us.

As you reflect on your own life, I encourage you to sit with these questions:

How have the challenges you've faced contributed to your personal growth and resilience?

_____

_____

_____

_____

_____

_____

_____

_____

_____

_____

_____

_____

_____

_____

In what ways do you experience God's unwavering love, even amidst your struggles and imperfections?

What steps can you take to embrace your past as a part of your story while moving forward into the promises of your future?

I challenge you to embrace your identity and pursue your best self, regardless of what others may say or the weight of your past. Remember that you are beautifully and wonderfully made, capable of achieving great things. Stand firm in the knowledge that no matter what happens in your life, God loves you fiercely and is always with you. Rise up! Take action Let your life be a reflection of the grace and love you have received. The well of redemption is waiting for you—drink deeply, and let it transform your life.

Last but not least, I want to leave you with some hope. To me, all this means nothing if you don't leave inspired and hopeful. My prayer is that through this book, you read something that will allow you to be able to find hope in your situation. Know that God is working it out, and no matter how jacked up it may seem nothing is too hard for God. In this season of my life. I find myself quoting scriptures more than anything. The one I find myself in all the time is **Psalms 23**. As I read this scripture it doesn't only speak to me. It speaks for me.

The Lord is my shepherd; I shall not want.

He maketh me to lie down in green pastures: he leadeth me beside the still waters.

He restoreth my soul: he leadeth me in the paths of righteousness for his name's sake.

Yea, though I walk through the valley of the shadow of death, I will fear no evil: for thou art with me; thy rod and thy staff they comfort me.

Thou preparest a table before me in the presence of mine enemies: thou anointest my head with oil; my cup runneth over.

Surely goodness and mercy shall follow me all the days of my life: and I will dwell in the house of the Lord forever.

Take a moment to reflect on your past and the journey that has shaped who you are today. Now, imagine you have the chance to write a letter to your younger self. In this letter embrace the concept of grace and forgiveness. Acknowledge the mistakes you made and the struggles you faced but also recognize that each experience contributed to your growth. Conclude your letter with words of encouragement, assuring your younger self that they are worthy of love and grace, just as they are. This letter will open a space for you to heal, so let the words and tears flow freely and authentically.

_____

_____

_____

_____

_____

_____

_____

_____

_____

_____

_____

References

Holy Bible, King James Version

About The Author

Tanzania Bacon

Tanzania Bacon is a dedicated mother of two sons, a passionate social worker, and a certified life coach and mentor. A proud graduate of Capella University with a degree in psychology, Tanzania combines her academic background with her life experiences to empower others. As an aunt, sister, and friend, she embodies the spirit of encouragement, always ready to uplift those around her.

Tanzania is the founder and owner of Built for Us, an agency committed to establishing healthy families by fostering foundational principles in faith, relationships, and finances. She believes in the importance of strong family dynamics and takes pride in guiding parents through life's transitions and obstacles, ensuring they feel supported every step of the way.

When she's not working, Tanzania enjoys spending quality time with her family, exploring new travel destinations, and engaging in competitive card games. Her spirited nature drives her to always strive for victory, whether in games or in life. Tanzania is not just a mentor; she's a hands-on leader who isn't afraid to get her hands dirty, walking alongside individuals and families as they build or rebuild the lives they desire. Her mission is to inspire, empower, and create lasting change within the communities she serves.

www.ingramcontent.com/pod-product-compliance
Lightning Source LLC
LaVergne TN
LVHW061039070526
838201LV00073B/5112